A COLORING BOOK ADVENTURE

SHERLOCK
THE MIND PALACE

SHERLOCK: THE MIND PALACE
A COLORING BOOK ADVENTURE

Copyright © 2015 by Mike Collins.

HarperCollins books may be purchased for educational, business, or sales promotional use.
For information please email the Special Markets Department at SPsales@harpercollins.com.

Published in 2015 by
Harper Design
An Imprint of HarperCollins*Publishers*
195 Broadway
New York, NY 10007
Tel: (212) 207-7000
Fax: (855) 746-6023
harperdesign@harpercollins.com
www.hc.com

Distributed throughout the world by
HarperCollins*Publishers*
195 Broadway
New York, NY 10007

ISBN 978-0-06-245837-7
Library of Congress Control Number: 2015949776

Printed in Canada

First Printing, 2015

Illustrations copyright © Mike Collins 2015

This book is published to accompany the television series entitled *Sherlock*
first broadcast on BBC One in 2010. *Sherlock* is a Hartswood Films production for
BBC Cymru Wales, co-produced with MASTERPIECE™.

Executive producers: Beryl Vertue, Mark Gatiss and Steven Moffat
Executive producer for the BBC: Bethan Jones
Executive producer for MASTERPIECE™: Rebecca Eaton
Series producer: Sue Vertue

All illustrations: Mike Collins with thanks to Rachael Stott

First published by BBC Books in 2015

SHERLOCK
THE MIND PALACE
MIKE COLLINS

HARPER
DESIGN
An Imprint of HarperCollinsPublishers

"YOU SEE, YOU JUST DON'T OBSERVE..."

Hidden within the illustrations are nine clues, essential to solving the crimes in each episode. The items are shown below, and the answers are given at the end of the book. Remember though, not every clue is hidden in the corresponding episode, so keep your wits about you...

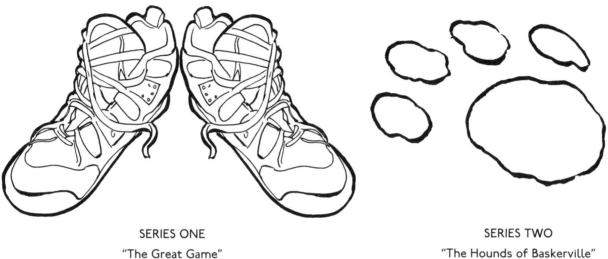

SERIES ONE

"The Great Game"

SERIES TWO

"The Hounds of Baskerville"

SERIES ONE

"A Study in Pink"

SERIES TWO

"The Reichenbach Fall"

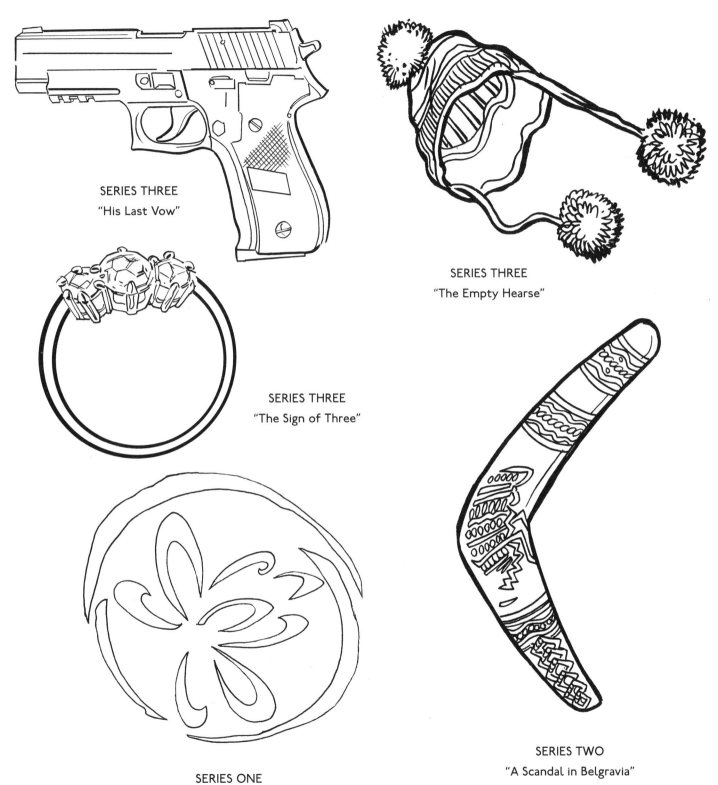

SERIES THREE
"His Last Vow"

SERIES THREE
"The Empty Hearse"

SERIES THREE
"The Sign of Three"

SERIES TWO
"A Scandal in Belgravia"

SERIES ONE
"The Blind Banker"

H.O.U.N.D.

LIberty, In

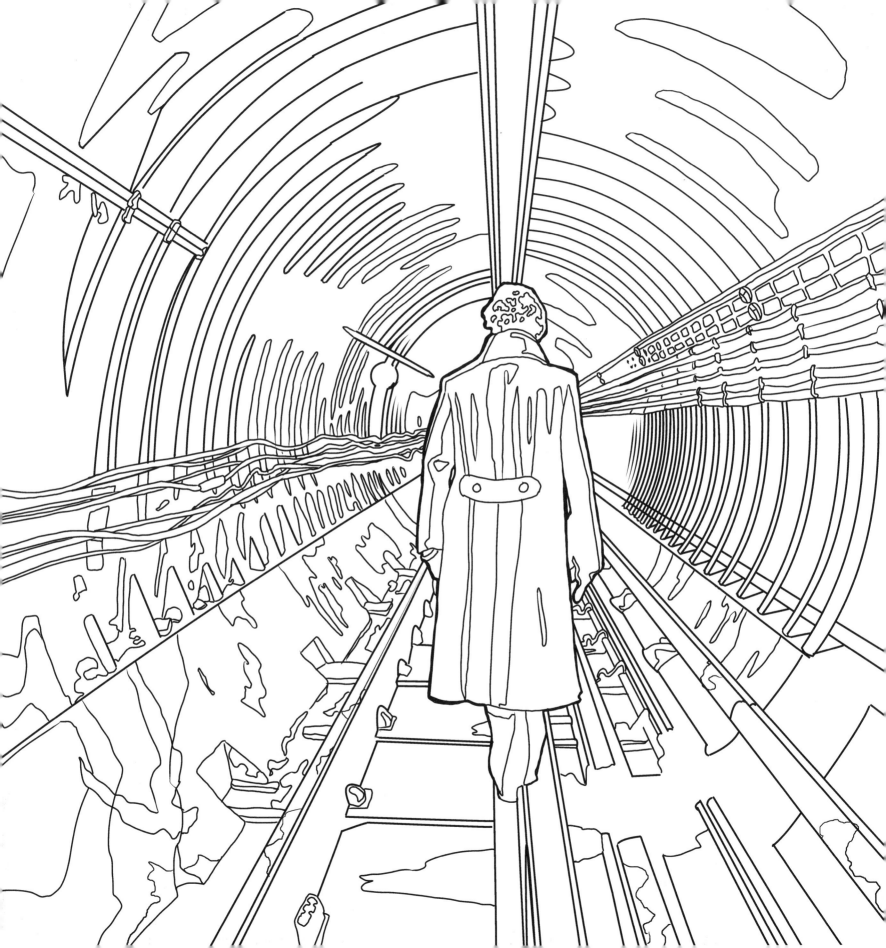

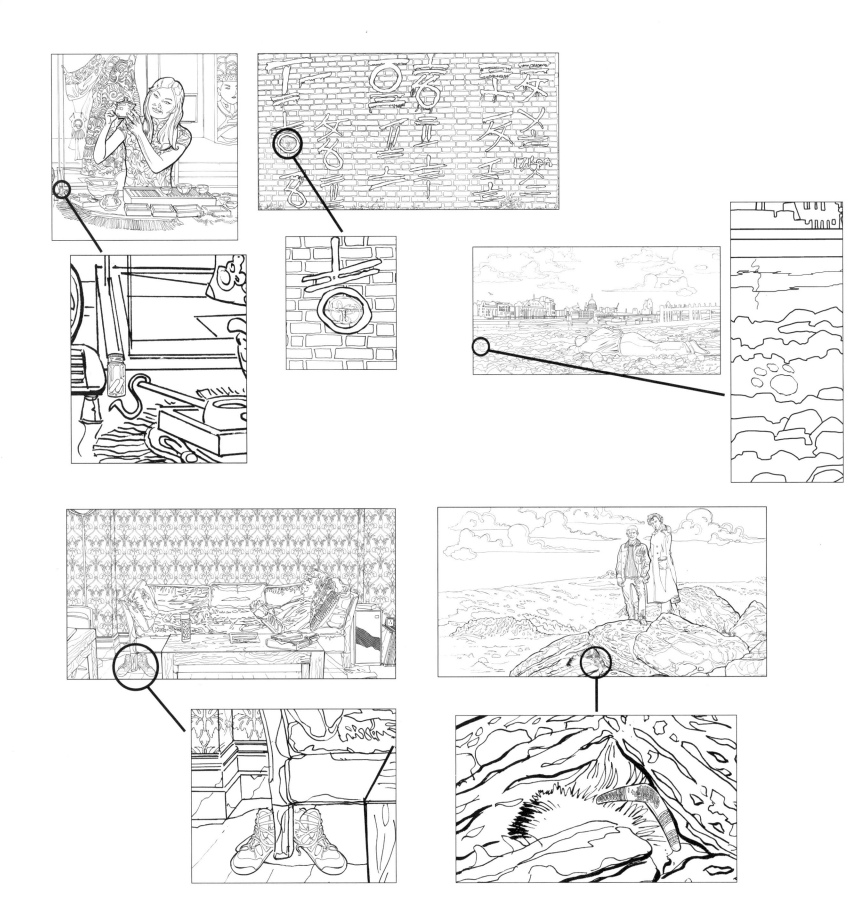

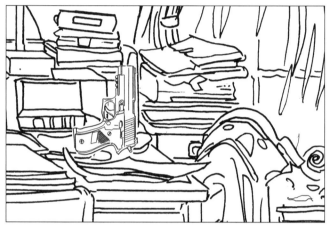